About the Author

Author is an exemplary figure of self-actualization in the IT industry, whose journey from a novice with no experience to reaching the heights of success at one of the largest IT companies inspires many. Starting his journey in the world of technology from scratch, Aleksandr not only navigated through numerous challenges and difficulties associated with entering the IT sphere but also acquired unique knowledge and skills that later formed the foundation of his professional success. Thanks to his perseverance, curiosity, and ability to learn quickly, Aleksandr rapidly advanced up the career ladder, moving from entry-level positions to top management in a leading IT company. His story is a testament to the fact that with the right approach and persistence, it's possible to achieve significant heights, even without initial experience in the field.

Having become a successful IT manager, Author decided that his life's mission was to help others achieve similar successes in their careers. He chose the path of a career consultant and mentor for top managers of IT companies, aiming to pass on his knowledge and experience to those at different stages of their professional journey in IT.

Author especially values the opportunity to work with young specialists who are just beginning their path in IT. He regularly introduces new specialists to the world of IT, helping them not only to find their first job but also to build a strategy for further career growth. Aleksandr is confident that everyone is capable of reaching significant heights if they find the strength to overcome initial difficulties and move consistently towards their goal.

Another key trait of Aleksandr as a mentor is his ability to see potential in people that they may not notice themselves. He has the skill to recognize hidden talents and abilities, encouraging specialists to develop and step beyond their usual perception of their capabilities. This feature makes him not just a mentor but a true mentor capable of changing someone's life for the better.

Through his book and professional activities, Aleksandr Gydyrym continues to inspire and support IT specialists on their path to success, contributing to the development of a new generation of leaders in the world of technology.

Chapter 1: First Steps in IT Management

Welcome to the world of IT management — a realm where innovation meets organization, and technology serves as a means to achieve business goals. This chapter is intended for those who are taking their first steps on the path to becoming an IT manager. We will look at the basics that will help you understand where to start and what skills need to be developed right now.

1.1 Understanding the Role of an IT Manager

Before diving into the study of specific skills and tools, it's important to understand what an IT manager actually does. This role requires not only deep technical knowledge but also the ability to manage projects, teams, and possess interpersonal communication skills.

IT managers play a key role in coordinating the work of developers, testers, designers, and other specialists to achieve the common goals of a project. They are responsible for planning, budgeting, prioritizing tasks, and ensuring timely completion of projects.

1.2 Skills Needed for Success

Successful management in the IT sphere requires both technical and soft skills. Here are some of the key skills you will need:

- **Technical Knowledge:** Understanding the basic principles of software development, systems analysis, and data management.
- **Project Management:** Knowledge of project management methodologies and tools, such as Agile, Scrum, or Kanban.
- **Communication Skills:** The ability to communicate effectively with teams, stakeholders, and clients.
- **Problem Solving:** The ability to analyze situations, find and implement solutions to complex issues.

In the following sections, we will delve more deeply into each of these skills and consider how to develop them.

1.3 Mastering Technical Knowledge

At the outset, it might seem that technical knowledge is an insurmountable barrier on the path to a career in IT management. However, in reality, mastering the basic technical principles and concepts is not only possible but also crucial for the successful management of projects and teams.

What to Study?

- **Programming Fundamentals:** Understanding at least one programming language, such as Python or JavaScript, will give you insight into the development processes and help in communicating with your development team.
- Systems Analysis and Design: Knowing the principles of system construction and architecture will help you better understand how IT projects work as a whole.
- Databases: Basics of working with databases are necessary to understand how data is stored, processed, and utilized in a project.

How to Study?

- **Online Courses and Webinars:** There are numerous online platforms, such as Coursera, Udemy, and edX, where you can find courses dedicated to programming fundamentals, systems analysis, and databases. Many of these courses are developed by leading universities and tech companies, ensuring high-quality material.

- **Self-learning:** The internet is filled with resources for self-learning. Blogs, forums, and YouTube tutorials can all be excellent aids in learning new information. The key here is not to be afraid to start and to be prepared that initially, much may seem unclear.

- **Practical Projects:** Start with small projects or even academic assignments that can help apply theoretical knowledge in practice. This could be creating a simple web application or working with a database. Real experience is what will truly help you understand how to apply the knowledge you've gained.

1.4 Project Management: First Steps

One of the key skills required for every IT manager is the ability to effectively manage projects. This includes planning, resource allocation, prioritizing tasks, and overseeing project execution.

Fundamentals of Project Management

- **Methodologies:** Learn about the main project management methodologies, such as Agile, Scrum, and Kanban. Each has its own features and advantages depending on the project type.

- **Project Management Tools:** There are many tools available that can help organize work on a project, such as Trello, Jira, and Asana. They will assist you in visualizing the work process, distributing tasks, and controlling deadlines.

- **Communication and Team Coordination:** Learn to communicate effectively with your team and coordinate their work. Regular meetings, clear task definitions, and feedback are key aspects of successful project management.

These first steps into the world of IT management are just the beginning of your journey. Ahead lie deep knowledge and practical skills that will not only make you a manager but a leader capable of leading a team and achieving high results.

As we delve further into the intricacies of IT management, the journey becomes more nuanced, requiring a blend of strategic thinking, technical prowess, and interpersonal skills to navigate the complexities of modern tech environments.

Chapter 2: Building Effective Teams in IT

2.1 The Anatomy of a Successful IT Team

The foundation of any successful IT project is a well-structured, cohesive team. But what makes a team effective? It's not just about gathering a group of skilled individuals; it's about creating a synergy where the collective output is greater than the sum of individual efforts.

Key Components of a Successful Team:

- Diversity: A mix of skills, backgrounds, and perspectives enhances creativity and problem-solving capabilities.
- Clear Roles and Responsibilities: Each team member understands their specific contributions and how they fit into the larger project.
- Open Communication: Encourage a culture where feedback is freely exchanged, and challenges are discussed openly without fear of retribution.
- Mutual Respect: Team members value each other's contributions and work collaboratively towards common goals.

2.2 Leadership in IT: More Than Just Management

In IT, leadership goes beyond mere project management. It's about inspiring your team, advocating for their needs, and driving innovation.

Becoming an Inspiring Leader:

- **Vision:** Share a clear, compelling vision of what the project aims to achieve and why it matters.

- **Empathy:** Understand the individual needs and motivations of your team members to foster a supportive environment.
- **Decisiveness:** Make informed decisions promptly and stand by them, creating a sense of stability and trust within the team.
- **Adaptability:** Be open to new ideas and willing to pivot strategies in response to changing circumstances or feedback.

2.3 Navigating Challenges in IT Projects

Even the best-planned projects can encounter unexpected challenges. From technical setbacks to scope creep, effective IT management involves anticipating potential problems and addressing them proactively.

Strategies for Overcoming Project Challenges:

- **Risk Management:** Regularly assess potential risks and develop contingency plans.
- **Stakeholder Engagement:** Keep stakeholders informed and involved, ensuring their expectations are aligned with the project's progress.
- **Agile Methodologies:** Incorporate agile practices to enhance flexibility and responsiveness to change.
- **Continuous Learning:** Encourage a culture of continuous improvement, where lessons learned from past projects are applied to future endeavors.

As you progress in your IT management career, remember that your role is multifaceted. You're not just overseeing projects but are instrumental in shaping the future of technology and innovation. By focusing on building effective teams, embodying inspiring leadership, and navigating project challenges with finesse, you'll set the stage for a rewarding and impactful career in IT management.

Chapter 3: Mastering Communication and Collaboration

3.1 Effective Communication in IT Projects

Communication is the lifeblood of any IT project. It's not just about conveying information; it's about ensuring clarity, understanding, and alignment among all team members and stakeholders.

Enhancing Communication Skills:

- **Active Listening:*** Encourage open dialogue and truly listen to team members' ideas and concerns.
- **Clear and Concise Messaging:** Avoid technical jargon when possible, especially when communicating with stakeholders unfamiliar with IT terminology.
- **Regular Updates:** Keep all parties informed about project progress, changes, and challenges to avoid surprises.

3.2 Fostering Collaboration in Diverse Teams

Collaboration in IT requires more than just working together; it involves leveraging each team member's strengths to achieve a common goal.

Strategies for Strengthening Team Collaboration:

- **Team-Building Activities:** Engage in exercises that build trust and mutual respect among team members.
- **Collaborative Tools:** Utilize project management and collaboration software to streamline workflows and enhance team synergy.
- **Conflict Resolution:** Address conflicts promptly and constructively, turning challenges into opportunities for team growth.

3.3 The Role of Emotional Intelligence in IT Management

Emotional intelligence (EI) is a crucial skill for IT managers, enabling them to navigate interpersonal dynamics effectively and lead with empathy.

Developing Emotional Intelligence:

- **Self-Awareness:** Understand your emotions, strengths, and weaknesses, and recognize their impact on others.
- **Social Awareness:** Be attentive to team members' feelings and perspectives, fostering an inclusive and supportive work environment.

- **Self-Regulation:** Manage your emotions and reactions, especially in high-pressure situations, to maintain professionalism and composure.
- **Relationship Management:** Build and maintain positive relationships within the team and with stakeholders, demonstrating empathy and understanding.

Chapter 4: Innovating and Leading Change

4.1 Embracing Innovation in IT Management

In the rapidly evolving tech landscape, staying ahead requires a commitment to innovation and a willingness to explore new ideas.

Cultivating an Innovative Mindset:

- **Encourage Experimentation:** Foster a culture where trial and error are seen as part of the learning process.
- **Stay Informed:** Keep up with the latest technology trends and consider how they can be applied to your projects.
- **Innovative Problem-Solving:** Encourage creative thinking when faced with challenges, exploring solutions beyond the conventional.

4.2 Leading Change in IT Projects

Change management is a critical aspect of IT management, involving guiding your team and stakeholders through transitions effectively.

Change Management Strategies:

- **Communicate the Vision:** Clearly articulate the reasons behind changes and the benefits they will bring.
- **Involve the Team:** Engage team members in the change process, soliciting their input and addressing concerns.
- **Build Momentum:** Celebrate small wins and progress towards the change, building confidence and enthusiasm.

4.3 Preparing for the Future of IT Management

As technology continues to advance, the role of the IT manager will also evolve. Staying adaptable and continuously learning are key to future success.

Future-Proofing Your IT Management Career:

- **Lifelong Learning:** Commit to ongoing education, whether through formal courses, seminars, or self-study.
- **Networking:** Build a strong professional network to share knowledge and stay abreast of industry developments.
- **Mentorship:** Seek mentors and become one yourself, fostering a culture of knowledge sharing and professional growth.

In conclusion, the journey to becoming an effective IT manager is continuous and multifaceted. By mastering communication, fostering collaboration, embracing innovation, and leading change, you'll not only navigate the complexities of the IT world but also pave the way for a future rich with opportunities and advancements.

Chapter 5: Strategic Thinking and Decision Making

5.1 Developing a Strategic Mindset

In the fast-paced world of IT, strategic thinking is not just a luxury; it's a necessity. It involves looking beyond the day-to-day operations and understanding the bigger picture of how technology can drive business success.

Key Elements of Strategic Thinking:

- **Visionary Outlook:** Being able to foresee future technology trends and their potential impact on the industry.
- **Analytical Skills:** Evaluating complex situations or challenges to identify the most effective solutions.
- **Innovation Focus:** Continually seeking innovative ways to improve processes, products, or services.

5.2 Effective Decision Making in IT

Decision-making in IT management requires a balance between speed and accuracy. It's about making informed choices that can lead to successful outcomes while mitigating risks.

Enhancing Decision-Making Skills:

- **Data-Driven Approach:** Utilize data and analytics to inform decisions, ensuring they are based on solid evidence.
- **Stakeholder Consideration:** Understand the needs and expectations of different stakeholders to guide decision-making processes.
- **Flexibility:** Be willing to adapt or change decisions as new information becomes available or circumstances change.

5.3 Navigating Complexity and Uncertainty

The IT landscape is characterized by its complexity and the constant uncertainty of technological evolution. Mastering the ability to navigate these aspects is crucial for any IT manager.

Strategies for Managing Complexity:

- **Simplification:** Break down complex projects or problems into manageable parts.
- **Collaboration:** Leverage the collective knowledge and skills of your team to tackle complex issues.

- **Continuous Learning:** Stay informed about new technologies and methodologies to better manage and anticipate changes.

Chapter 6: Cultivating Resilience and Adaptability

6.1 Building Resilience in IT Teams

Resilience is the capacity to recover quickly from difficulties. In the context of IT, this means ensuring your team can adapt and continue to perform under changing or challenging conditions.

Fostering a Resilient Team Culture:

- **Supportive Environment:** Create a supportive atmosphere where team members feel valued and understood.
- **Encourage Flexibility:** Promote a mindset of flexibility and openness to change among team members.
- **Develop Problem-Solving Skills:** Equip your team with the skills and resources they need to effectively solve problems.

6.2 Embracing Adaptability as a Core Competency

In an industry that evolves at lightning speed, adaptability is a critical competency for any IT manager. It's about embracing change and leading your team through transitions with confidence.

Ways to Enhance Adaptability:

- **Stay Curious:** Foster a culture of curiosity and continuous learning within your team.
- **Experiment Often:** Encourage experimentation and risk-taking in pursuit of innovation and improvement.
- **Embrace Failure:** View failures as opportunities for growth and learning, rather than setbacks.

In conclusion, the journey through IT management is both challenging and rewarding. By focusing on strategic thinking, decision-making, navigating complexity, and cultivating resilience and adaptability, you'll not only keep pace with the rapidly evolving tech landscape but also lead your team to new heights of success.

Chapter 7: Fostering Innovation and Continuous Improvement

7.1 Creating an Innovation-Driven Culture

Innovation is not just about having one or two breakthrough ideas; it's about creating an environment where innovation can flourish continuously. An innovation-driven culture encourages experimentation, values creativity, and embraces change as an opportunity for growth.

Strategies for Cultivating Innovation:

- **Empowerment:** Give team members the autonomy to explore new ideas and take ownership of their projects.
- **Reward Creativity:** Recognize and reward innovative solutions and risk-taking, even if every initiative doesn't lead to success.
- **Collaborative Spaces:** Encourage cross-functional collaboration to spark diverse perspectives and innovative solutions.

7.2 Implementing Continuous Improvement Processes

Continuous improvement is a perpetual effort to enhance products, services, or processes. In IT management, this means constantly seeking ways to increase efficiency, reduce waste, and improve quality and customer satisfaction.

Key Aspects of Continuous Improvement:

- **Feedback Loops:** Establish mechanisms for regular feedback from both customers and team members to inform ongoing improvements.
- **Lean Principles:** Apply lean methodologies to streamline processes, eliminate inefficiencies, and maximize value.
- **Agile Practices:** Embrace agile practices to enhance adaptability and responsiveness to change.

7.3 Leveraging Technology for Innovation

Technology itself is a powerful tool for fostering innovation. By staying ahead of technological trends and leveraging the latest tools, IT managers can drive significant advancements and competitive advantages.

Technology Trends to Watch:

- **Artificial Intelligence and Machine Learning:** Harness AI and ML to automate processes, enhance decision-making, and create personalized customer experiences.
- **Cloud Computing:** Utilize cloud services for flexibility, scalability, and cost-efficiency.
- **Cybersecurity:** Prioritize cybersecurity innovations to protect data and maintain trust.

Chapter 8: Leading High-Performing IT Teams

8.1 Building and Sustaining High-Performing Teams

High-performing teams are the cornerstone of successful IT projects. Creating such teams requires a deliberate approach to recruitment, development, and leadership.

Elements of High-Performing IT Teams:

- **Clear Goals and Objectives:** Ensure every team member understands their role in achieving the team's goals.
- **Strong Leadership:** Provide visionary leadership that motivates and inspires team members to perform at their best.
- **Open Communication:** Foster an environment of transparency and open communication.

8.2 Nurturing Talent and Professional Growth

Investing in the professional growth of your team members is critical for maintaining a high-performing team. Continuous learning opportunities, mentorship, and career development paths are key.

Strategies for Talent Development:

- **Personalized Development Plans:** Work with team members to identify career goals and create personalized development plans.
- **Mentorship Programs:** Establish mentorship programs to facilitate knowledge transfer and leadership development.

- **Learning Opportunities:** Provide access to training, workshops, and conferences to keep skills sharp and knowledge current.

In wrapping up, the journey through IT management is ongoing and dynamic. By fostering innovation, pursuing continuous improvement, leveraging technology, and leading high-performing teams, you'll not only navigate the complexities of the tech world but also shape its future. This book is your compass in that journey, guiding you to become an effective leader who can inspire change, drive progress, and achieve lasting success in the ever-evolving IT landscape.

Let's continue our journey through the landscape of IT management with a focus on the critical elements that facilitate sustainable growth and leadership.

Chapter 9: Leveraging Data for Strategic Insights

9.1 The Power of Data Analytics

In the digital age, data is often referred to as the new oil. For IT managers, leveraging data analytics can provide deep insights into customer behavior, operational efficiency, and market trends.

Harnessing Data for Decision-Making:

- **Data-Driven Culture:** Cultivate an environment where decisions are made based on data rather than intuition.
- **Analytics Tools:** Utilize advanced analytics tools to interpret complex datasets, revealing patterns and insights that were not apparent before.
- **Predictive Modeling:** Apply predictive models to forecast future trends, enabling proactive adjustments to strategies.

9.2 Ensuring Data Quality and Integrity

The reliability of data-driven decisions is directly tied to the quality of the data. Ensuring data integrity is paramount for any organization that aims to make informed decisions.

Strategies for Maintaining Data Quality:

- **Regular Audits:** Implement routine checks to ensure data accuracy and consistency.
- **Data Governance Policies:** Establish clear data governance policies that outline how data is collected, stored, and maintained.
- **Training and Awareness:** Educate team members on the importance of data quality and the role they play in maintaining it.

Chapter 10: Scaling IT Operations for Growth

10.1 Strategic Scaling of IT Infrastructure

As organizations grow, so too does the demand on their IT infrastructure. Strategic scaling involves not just expanding capacity but also optimizing for efficiency and agility.

Key Considerations for Scaling:

- **Cloud Computing:** Leverage cloud solutions for scalable and flexible IT infrastructure.
- **Automation:** Automate routine tasks to improve efficiency and reduce the risk of human error.
- **Modular Design:** Adopt a modular approach to system design, allowing for easier updates and scalability.

10.2 Managing Risks in Scaling

Expansion brings new challenges and risks, particularly in the realms of security and system stability. Managing these risks is crucial to ensure uninterrupted operations.

Risk Management Strategies:

- **Comprehensive Security Measures:** Implement robust security protocols, including regular updates and patches to protect against cyber threats.
- **Load Testing:** Conduct load testing to assess the system's performance under various stress conditions, ensuring stability during peak usage.
- **Disaster Recovery Planning:** Develop a disaster recovery plan to quickly restore operations in the event of a system failure or data breach.

Conclusion: Shaping the Future of IT Management

The role of an IT manager is multifaceted, requiring a delicate balance between technical expertise, strategic vision, and leadership acumen. By leveraging data for strategic insights, scaling operations thoughtfully, and navigating the complexities of modern IT environments, you can drive your organization toward sustainable growth and innovation.

As technology continues to evolve, so too will the challenges and opportunities it presents. Staying agile, continually learning, and embracing change are not just strategies for success but imperatives for survival and prosperity in the dynamic world of IT management.

This book aims to be a guide on your journey, offering insights, strategies, and inspiration to navigate the ever-changing IT landscape with confidence and skill. Remember, the future of IT is not just about managing technology but about leading with vision and empowering others to achieve their full potential.

As a bonus, I offer you a checklist shuffle on how to achieve success for both beginners and experienced professionals in job hunting. This checklist, provides clear instructions and emphasizes the critical role of crafting a compelling resume—a theme that will be thoroughly explored in my next book. Here's an outline:

Job Hunting Success Checklist

Understanding Your Goals:
- Identify your career objectives and what you seek in your next role.
- Reflect on your skills and how they align with your career aspirations.

Skills and Experience:
- List your technical skills, leadership experiences, and achievements.
- Match your skills with job requirements in your desired IT field.

Networking and Mentorship:
- Engage with professionals in your desired IT sector through networking events, online forums, and social media.
- Seek mentorship from experienced individuals in the IT management field.

Learning and Development:
- Highlight any ongoing or completed courses relevant to IT management.
- Showcase certifications or projects that demonstrate your commitment to continuous learning.

Crafting Your Resume:
- Ensure your resume clearly articulates your skills, experiences, and achievements.
- Tailor your resume for each application to align with the job's specific requirements.
- (**Note:** Crafting a compelling resume is crucial for making a strong first impression. Dive deeper into this topic in my upcoming book dedicated to creating effective resumes.)

Preparing for Interviews:
- Research the company and the role you're applying for thoroughly.
- Prepare responses to common interview questions and articulate how your background aligns with the job.

Follow-up and Feedback:
- Always send a thank-you email after interviews.
- Seek feedback on your application or interview, regardless of the outcome.

This checklist serves as a guide to navigating the complexities of the job market in the IT industry. For a more detailed exploration of creating a resume that stands out and catches the attention of top IT companies, look forward to my upcoming book. It will not only complement the insights provided here but will also equip you with the knowledge to craft resumes that open doors to exciting career opportunities.

Remember, the journey to finding your ideal job in IT is a strategic one, requiring careful planning, continuous improvement, and a standout resume. Stay tuned for my next book, which will delve into the art of resume writing, helping you secure your next role in the IT industry.

Unlock Your Dream IT Job:
Pre-Order and Transform Your Resume Today

Unlock the secrets to landing your dream IT job with **"How to Craft Your Key to Success: The Ultimate Guide to Resume Writing for IT Professionals."** In today's competitive job market, a standout resume is not just a necessity—it's your first step toward success. This comprehensive guide goes beyond the basics, offering you insider tips, strategies, and techniques tailored specifically for the IT industry.

From understanding what IT hiring managers are looking for to highlighting your technical skills and achievements in the most compelling way, this book covers it all. Learn how to:

- Navigate the nuances of IT-specific resume writing, including how to present complex projects and technical skills.
- Use psychological triggers that make your resume stand out from the stack.
- Tailor your resume for different IT roles, from entry-level positions to executive leadership.
- Leverage the power of keywords and SEO to ensure your resume is discovered online.
- Avoid common pitfalls that can send your resume straight to the rejection pile.

But that's not all—pre-order now and gain exclusive access to hidden content that delves deeper into personal branding, crafting a winning LinkedIn profile, and strategies for leveraging your network during the job hunt. These secrets, reserved only for early buyers, will give you an unbeatable edge in your IT career journey.

Don't let your resume be the barrier between you and your next IT role. "How to Craft Your Key to Success" is more than just a book; it's your blueprint to making a lasting impression and securing the job of your dreams. Pre-order today and take the first step toward transforming your career.

www.ingramcontent.com/pod-product-compliance
Lightning Source LLC
Chambersburg PA
CBHW040311220526
45473CB00002B/631